# Workbook

## Christopher Merrill

TEAL PRESS
Santa Fe, New Mexico

*For Lisa*

## Acknowledgements

Some of these poems were first published in *Cincinnati Poetry Review, Denver Quarterly, Kingfisher, New Virginia Review, Oxford Magazine, Peagasus, Poetry Northwest, Quarterly West, Rhino,* and *Seattle Review.*

Copyright © 1988 by Christopher Merrill
Printed in the United States of America
Library of Congress Catalog Card Number: 88-51507
ISBN 0-913793-09-4

Book Design: Robert Jebb
Author Photo: Mark Kane

Teal Press
P.O. Box 4098
Santa Fe, New Mexico 87502

Teal Press Books are sewn for binding durability
and printed on acid-free paper for longevity.

# Workbook

# Contents

## IV  The Sea

# The Guests

Now in the evening, the guests rub the lead
Glass in the window, and watch the moon dissolve.
Out back, an old man bends a guitar string
Around the silver light, tuning the air
To the slick sounds of rain, to the high clouds
That gather there at dusk and disappear
Before the wind rises, and to the flashing
Of fireflies trapped in the heat, in the milk bottles
On the porch, where a sleeping child is dreaming
Of llamas and lutes . . .
                              And if the earth begins
To hum, and the dry wells refill themselves,
The guests may close their eyes, and sing.

# I
# Lessons

# Childhood

Newspapers scarred the stream;
Words swirled in the eddies;
Grey figures—a dead thief,
The President and his wife,
Two race horses—floated past
And sank . . .
                Or snagged the rocks
Rippling the slow water
Until the sun, like a man
With a knife, cut them apart
So they could sail away.

———————

On the last night, outside my tent, someone
Startled the woods: a flashlight fluttered; twigs,
Like small animals, crackled underfoot;
Mosquitoes buzzed the netting. I held my breath
To hear the hushed voices, a muffled cough,
A siren down the road . . .
                    A match was struck.
I crawled outside: my mother and my father,
Dressed in white, stood near the sumac, waving
Their hands of fire. They touched the trees, they licked
Their palms, and rose above the burning woods.

# Crossing the Bridge

A sleek shell emerges
From the fog on the water,
Like a thought becoming clear.
The bridge drifts in the wind.

A dark-haired man divides
The air with long, sure strokes
Until the smooth water opens
Like a cut, and we see the bones

Of the lake... My mother winces,
The bridge hums, and three ducks,
Swimming in a V, take to flight,
Squawking, necks outstretched.

The bridge sags underfoot.
The sculler turns, sweeping
The water with one oar—
Like my father mopping blood

Off the floor as my mother
Bundled me into the car—
Then glides away, trailing
A string of light behind.

# Fable

How the gravestones smiled!
And clouds, like flowers,
Settled over the trees
In arrangements of grey,
When I hid on the hill
To watch my funeral.

My mother, in sackcloth
And ashes and at attention
(Minister's orders), wept
Until my father hoisted
My casket up into an opening
In the clouds, where it floated

Among the swirling leaves
And shadows, like a sheath
Of bark launched on a stream—
It was then she laughed,
And cast her flowers overhead,
And danced a jig around my grave...

And when he gave my casket
A push, and it sailed to the sun,
And I rolled down the hill
To follow the chosen one,
She joined the crowd in silence,
Tears hardening on her lips.

## A Boy Juggling A Soccer Ball

after practice: right foot
to left foot, stepping forward and back,
   to right foot and left foot,
and left foot up to his thigh, holding
   it on his thigh as he twists
around in a circle until it rolls
   down the inside of his leg,
like a tickle of sweat, now catching
   and tapping on the soft
side of his foot, and juggling
   once, twice, three times,
hopping on one foot like a jump-roper
   in the gym, now trapping
and holding the ball in mid-air,
   balancing it on the instep
of his weak left foot, stepping forward
   and forward and back, then lifting
it overhead until it settles in the air;
   and squaring off his body,
he keeps the ball aloft with a nudge
   of his neck, heading it
from side to side, softer and softer,
   like the fading refrain
on an old 45, until the ball balances
   itself on his hairline,
the hot sun and sweat filling his eyes
   as he jiggles this way
and that, then flicking it up gently,
   hunching his shoulders
and tilting his head back, he traps it
   in the hollow of his neck,
and bending at the waist, sees his shadow,
   his dangling T-shirt, the bent
blades of brown grass in summer heat;
   and relaxing, the ball slipping
down his back . . . and missing his foot.

He wheels around, he marches
over the ball, as if it were a rock
    he'd stumbled into, and pressing
his left foot against it, he pushes it
    against the inside of his right
until it pops into the air, is heeled
    over his head—the rainbow!—
and settles on his extended thigh before
    rolling over his knee and down
his shin, so he can juggle it again
    from his left foot to his right foot
—and right foot to left foot to thigh—
    as he wanders, on the last day
of summer, around the empty field.

## Concert

When the catalpa's seedpods drop
At dusk and harden into drumsticks,
A child hears, against the curb,
The leaves' brush strokes; and, underfoot,
The chestnuts click like castanets
Until a bell ushers him in.

Soon the wind's curtains rise; and branches,
Like bows, scrape his bedroom window,
Introducing the simple cadences
Of rain, the syncopation of hail,
And the storm's measure, to the boy,
Who drums his fingers on the sill,

Keeping time.

# Children's Suite

I *Seaglass*

Buffed in the ocean's tumbler,
Polished with seawrack and sand,
Rolled and lulled like dice
Around the North Atlantic,—
It bears the voices of sailors,
Of men and women shrieking
In the game rooms and cabins
Of sinking ships, of the sea
Itself, to the deaf child
Collecting shells at low tide.

II *Tongue-Tied*

I forgive my tongue's clipped wings,
The rusted scissors, the nod;
The cluttered kitchen table
On which they laid me down;
The smoke in the doctor's eyes;
The bourbon shaking his hand;
My father, who fainted twice;
And my mother, flecked with blood,
Who should have known better;
For my blood tasted like milk,
A birdcall swelled in my throat,
And my first words let me fly.

III  *First Questions*

Whose eyes rolled my shadow
Into a little ball? Whose heart
Bounced it to the window?
Whose breath let it fall
To the ground? And whose feet
Dribbled it down the street
Until the child fishing
For snakes in the gutter
Received it from the leaves
And passed it to his father,
Who let it fall to pieces
Before the sun went down?


IV  *Correspondences*

The stems of seven daffodils
Leaning against the lip of the glass,
Like the pencils, bolts, and nails
That filled the mason jars
Lining my father's workbench,
Unravel near the top, and hide
In the bowed heads of the flowers,
Like the cigarettes that grew
Out of his mouth, and nose, and ears
On Sundays, driving home from church.

# The Parade: July 4th, 1970

Where the main road disappeared
Around a bend of trees and boulders—
Washed downhill in the last storm—firemen
Carried our village with them: floats,
Horses and guns, a marching band . . .
But the road, like a shallow stream
Boys will tramp across, cleared again.

Then nine young men, dressed in black robes,
Barefoot and hooded in the heat,
Followed their elders through the town,
An empty coffin on their shoulders.
Silenced by the procession, our porches
Crackled once the light-soaked road
Swallowed the chanting men and the coffin.

# The Fishing Jacket

*for Lyall Merrill 1902-1970*


Folded and wrinkled and mothballed
In a *Salvation Army* box, his khaki jacket
Reeking of salmon eggs . . . When I shake it out, flecks
Settle in the musty closet, like cinders,
And the leaders of black thread
Dangling in the empty button holes begin to shiver.
A tuft of feathers brushes past—too small
For birds, his tied flies crumble in my hands.

And on the shelf by the cracked window, an urn
Filled with his ashes: *He was*
*Such a little man,* my grandmother had said
After the service, passing the urn
Back to the minister—and everyone had laughed . . .

Now when his sleeves cover my hands, I, too, must laugh.

————————

In my war dream, I wear
A field commander's coat. World War II. Near the front lines
In North Africa, where Rommel's scent
Is faint, and General Patton's spilled his bourbon
In our tent again . . . Outside, the desert sun
Pricks my skin like a sewing needle, stitching my memory
Into the sand.
                        I drift. I unravel
A cigarette, and let the French tobacco fly in the wind.
*Our casualties,* I tell the good general,
*Have been heavy.* He nods, and smiles, then stares at me
—At the name splayed across my breast pocket—
And I hold my breath, believing
He can keep a secret . . .

————————

*I put her out of her pain*
Was the first line of my first song. I sang
My six-year-old triumph at dusk, at the frayed edge
Of my grandfather's orchard, where my cairn
Of bricks balanced on top of a red-winged blackbird
—With a broken wing—was swaying in the wind,
Where I heard a faint trill, a sad song,
Catch and die in her dying throat . . .

*No,* he muttered, *not like that!*
And slipped the bricks off one by one.
He cupped the bird in his large, yellow, shaking hands,
He dusted her wings, he set her in the bushes. *She'll heal
Herself,* he said, and marched me up the hill.

And I, who had already returned from the dead
Nine times before dinner, who knew Death
Lasts only as long as it takes to climb
A tree and hide from your enemies,
Your slow friends, believed him . . .

In the morning, flies pinned
Like medals to my blackbird's wings, I gripped
The rusted belt girding an apple tree,
Hoisted myself up onto its cement sealer,
And hid in the leaves from the sky,
Which knows my song by heart.

———————

And when I open the window, two plates of glass
Slide down the ivy, and fall into the garden
Without breaking . . .

*Scatter the ashes, and wait,* I tell myself. *Wait.*

# Lessons

In the Sunday *Times:* a spread of photographs
From the Lodz ghetto, grainy takes of the end—
I stare and stare at a locksmith: the key
Is his six-pointed star. These are the steps
No one can climb, this the soup line, and this
The *babka* made of ground potato peels—
And here's an advertisement: *Take a good
Long look . . .* A woman in a white silk shirt
(Stamped and numbered on the order form)
Clutches her belt, smiling for the camera.

———————

What could I learn from you whose bruisings bore
The imprints of shoes and phones? who turned my back
Into a checkered map of dog brush marks?
Who made my wrists and fingers swell, like balloons . . .
Begetters of my silence and my wrath,
I learned from your refrain—*If I have to,
I'll beat the truth out of you!*—to lie, to speak
In signs (*Don't touch!*), to whisper and hide; and then
How hard it is to untie myself from you
When I wind these words around our common wounds.

———————

The snap and rise and dip of my sidearm
Slider, the whistle of my sucker pitch
Sweeping the spring air clean, the ancient wish
Of my stone whirring across the field—these caught
Him in the eye. . . *Because I did, because
He cheated us again, because I had it
In my hand*—Mr. Chrenko took my hand,
Spat out a Yiddish curse, then twisted my arm
Around the light I'd stolen from his son,
Condemning me to a life of wandering.

# II
# Notes For A Self-Portrait

# Sacrilege

These are my credentials: I traveled
To Egypt when I was a younger man
And tunneled into a pyramid.

With a rope tied to a rock
By the entrance, I picked my way
Through the dust and rubble for the better

Part of a week until I found—
In the corner of a false tomb, under
A pile of stones—the passage to the burial room.

Paintings covered the walls:
Harvest time, hunting, the sacrifice
Of animals. Twelve alabaster

Vases surrounded a sarcophagus,
Where a mummified king slept
A serpentine sleep. . .

I chiseled the ivory and gold
From his wooden furniture, slipped the silver
Jewelry off his arms and legs, smashed

His pottery against the walls. Then
I followed the rope back to safety
And sailed to England. . .

Now when I say I stole my eyes
From the dead, just remember one thing:
I'm the thief you sent for.

# Poaching

*"You'd have to be able... to see*
*what steals I've made and used."—Charles Wright*


At dusk, in the rusted light of August, I hummed like a wire
Along the fence dividing the widow's land
Into thirds, into the past,
                    present, and future perfect
Tenses of the verb *to have* in its holy trinity
Of greed, and skimmed
               my voice across the pond, the warm air,
The waves and watery tops of timothy and alfalfa,
To scare her horses imported from Russia
             and the black men poaching in our woods.

---

In Fergus Tufts' field, shucking ears of corn
And whistling through the skins: a buck and a doe,
Feeding nearby, looked up, and didn't scare
Until I slipped away, the stalks stripped clean,
Our dinner tucked underarm, like a newspaper.

And when I climbed the bridle path, holding
The fence to keep from sliding down the muck,
The gully of horseshoes, and broken rails,
And cigarette butts scuffed into hoofprints,
A host of spirits tracked me through the woods,

Singing a song of the grief stitched, like stripes,
Into the fabric of my innocent needs.

---

Thus a scattering of seeds plundered from memory's husk—

At noon, through the trees, the way the light's riptide
and roll confuse the story line:

A bundle of oil-soaked rugs, or the smell of singed flesh;

Names like Clarence Nagro, "Mad" Anthony Wayne, Tempe Wick;

A horse hidden in a bedroom, corn and apples rotting under
the floorboards, and soldiers plotting in the snow;

A barn fire and Tanya's stallions galloping into the sky;—

And then, at dusk, the way the round heads of red clover
bob in the wind, marking the far side of silence.

———————————

"If you mean to kill me, shoot me now!"
Cried General Wayne, opening his coat. "Here's
My heart." And his drunken soldiers reeled away
With fixed bayonets, fifes and drums, the cannon,
And a hundred head of cattle from the compound—
His Pennsylvania Line, knee-deep in snow,
Veering barefoot between Vealtown and Princeton.

New Year's night, 1781—
Talbot and Bettin dead; Henry Wick's daughter
Stopped on the road, then followed home (her horse,
To the men's chagrin, vanishing along the way);
And now, an unpaid month of building and
Rebuilding huts and redoubts ending in
Revolt, a volley fired—overhead—at him . . .

Still, he chose to ride with them, who'd lived
On dogs, birch bark, roasted shoes. "Their business was
With Congress"—not with him. They'd worshipped him,
Like sons, this band of laborers and bounty-
Seekers; and so, like the helpless father who
Must watch his children make their own mistakes,
He headed for Princeton and imprisonment...

———————

For memory invents its own network of new connections—

At daybreak, from the footbridge, I watched Tanya's friend
lead a white horse down to the stream, and shoot it.

All afternoon the stench of rotting flesh staining the air,
the swamp grass, the stones.

"...Because Clarence is illiterate," my father explained,
explaining nothing.

But when the rank water filled our pond, the clouds' boats
sailed past without signaling, stranding me there.

And when their barn burned down that fall, I saw a fleet of
slave ships blazing in a distant harbor.

— Then I heard the beginning and the end of speech and song

———————

But here invention flags before the facts:
When Sam Tufts (volunteer fire chief, Babe Ruth
Team coach, and plumber) choked a black-robed boy
One Fourth of July, honoring the war
In Asia and the memory of his nephew—
Fergus' son—by protesting the students'
Protest of our parade (their coffin lay
In pieces near the judges' stand), the sun
Burned through the fittings in the clouds, and burst
Into the students' song... Soon a horse-van came
To spirit them away, and the firemen raised
Their hands. My first pitch rattled the batting cage.

---

Smoke drifted overhead. The woods blazed
With signs: scars on a stranger's face. And when the last thread
Of light broke in the sky, and a gust of wind
Swept the smoke away, I knelt in the blackberry brambles
And wept. I licked my wrists. Tasted juice. Blood. Then footsteps,
Voices whispering beyond the fence, and my heart,
Like a fist, opening in the dark,
To lead me home again.

## The Diver

was balanced on the edge of the platform
when a word appeared like a moon, gathered in clouds,
and swirled above his hands and eyes—he jumped
upwards and out, tucking his legs and head
into his body's shell and, somersaulting
backwards, searching the ceiling for a polestar,
he cracked his skull on the platform, nicking
the dormant seed of his own death, and dropped
feet first, head slumped, slicing through the air,
the water, bleeding from his mouth and ears,
to root himself on the bottom of the pool
and see the springboards fluttering in their sheaths,
the whole crowd on their feet, speaking in tongues,
a woman waving a broken fist or a flower,
then a light rising through the crimson water:
the sun the sailor takes his warning from.

# The Gatekeeper
### *after Kafka*

Awake again at the twisted iron gate,
Where the Chinese girl is still on guard. To enter
The city, in which I hope to find the lost
Messenger, I must sign my name on her
Black silk skirt. But my names, my various
Signatures, never seem to work. Thus I offer
New ones: Savonarola, Gabriel
Fahrenheit, William Cody—she smiles, but no.

To keep her attention (she's easily distracted),
I tell her about the blind pianist
Who hammered his black keys together, nailing
His hymn to my door, like an old wreath, I even
Hum a few bars. She leans against the gate,
Wincing. As usual, the glittering mosques
In the distance prompt me to repeat my story
About the freighters lighting up the harbor:

How they change into candles at midnight;
How they burn their iron wicks, turning the water
To wax; and how, as the bridge begins to melt,
The cars dissolve into the vanishing road;—
She sighs, as if to say, *It's come to this?*
*There I am!* I cry. *On a mountaintop. Fasting.*
*While General Sherman marches to the sea.*
She raises an eyebrow, considering.

*His armies leave a trail of smoke behind,*
I continue, my confidence mounting, *and the tears*
*Of women after rape. The defeated soldiers*
*Stand apart, heads down, shoeless and drunk . . .*
For some reason, when I notice she's smiling again,
I lose my place, I begin to falter: *Horses*
*With burning eyes are neighing in the night—*
She frowns. So I hurry on, ignoring her:

*I hear a steady drumbeat in the wind.*
*I've been there now a week, and nothing's changed.*
*Nothing will change*—she starts to walk away.
*Wait!* I plead. She stops just long enough
For me to remind her about the sacred
Fish rotting in the artist's studio;
The hourglass opening its mouth to let
The sand return to the sea; the desperadoes

In the Badlands who held up my westbound coach
And left me in the road, like a rattlesnake
Coiled on a riverbank;—and then she's gone . . .
Once again, I drop to my knees, and on
The scrap of silk she always leaves behind,
I paint exactly what I see—the red
Sun surrounded by its twelve silver knives—
Then wait for the horses, the wild horses, to come.

# Three Poems

I  *Apartments*

Autumn's scaffold draws no crowd today;
Yet the last leaves of ivy, clinging
To the brick like the fingers of a washerwoman
Wringing old clothes dry, bind the windows
Of strangers together in a blaze
Of red, when the sun threads the mountains
In the distance, and hitches the land to the sky.


II  *The Knot*

A piece of string tied around a tree.
The tree's knotted with disease. A man
Unties the string, and holds it in his hands.
As it grows heavy, he lies down.
He drapes it over his chest, spreading
His arms wide. Clouds cover the sun, then pass,
And his lips, his closed eyes, hold the new light.


III  *Last Rites*

After the guests and their goodbyes dissolve
Into the cold, white air, the widow draws
The curtains, and trims the candlewicks, ruffling
The shadows on the floor. *Sleep, sleep,* she whispers.
Then she lifts the coffin's lid, its veil, arranges
The wreath around her husband's chest, and rubs
His body till the shadows turn away.

## Beliefs

*for Larry Levis*


When the foghorn slashed through the morning, the mist
Bled into the sea, and the wind, baring
Its fists again, bruised the shoreline and the wharves.
Then the freighters held their breath, like businessmen,
And, skirting the point, disappeared, leaving
Unguents of oil to salve the mangled piers.

———————

What's important? Stones, beliefs, the blue
Eyes of the woman on the beach, who rode
Her horse to the Dead Sea, who kissed you—once...
Say she wore a leather coat, or changed
The color of the clouds, or said she loved you—
What's important is the way she left...

———————

Banish the sea—and the wind, like a frightened child,
Will hug the wavering shore until the sea
Returns...And if you ruin the wind, horses
Will canter through the mud, blinding their riders...
But cut the horses' throats—and the old words
Will lose their riders, the wind, and the sea again.

# The Rope

At the end of the tunnel, where the red light hums, saltwater twists
me into the sand.

I smell your ancient perfume in the hair of the walls.

I watch your hands open, then close a large oak door; and when
I open that door, I discover a rope hanging from a bridge a mile
overhead.

I climb the rope, hoisting myself up hand over hand, swinging
around in a circle, till you lean over the railing and smile—then cut
the rope!

Just before I hit the water, the river freezes over and my body,
as it cracks the ice, crumbles into a dream of myself...

The door slams shut. The light shatters, the melting ice evaporates.

Crying, clinging to the wall, I crawl out of the tunnel...only
to find you again, walking up a city street.

Your eyes, when you turn away, burn black—before you
disappear, leaving on the sidewalk a trail of charcoal.

A trail I follow out of the city and into the hills, into the forest,
where a plume of smoke singes my tongue, granting me the power
of speech.

And there you are, in a clearing—surrounded by candles!

I reach for you, begging for light and water.

I know my life will end like this.

# Notes for a Self-Portrait

1.  Seven finger-splints lined up on my desk, like shotgun shells.
2.  Harvesting teeth from the tilled field of my divisions
    and departures.
3.  My loose tongue slipping out of its clothes again.
4.  A frayed rope of words looped over an ivy-covered wall.
5.  A gold piece and a wish—and then another wish.
6.  Two stones drying on the windowsill . . . Or: the oxen
    yoked together by a pair of spectacles.
7.  The scar sinking into my brow, like dirt settling in a grave.
8.  The tangled roots of the cedar toppled in the windstorm
    yielding to the practice of the aspen healing over its
    initialed wounds.
9.  Ears that hear bells cracking in the square and the small
    explosions of the clock.
10. Then a charred voice rising out of the ashes of
    another life, another world, whispering *Now begin.*

# III
# Work Songs

# Work Songs

*for my father*

## I   *Clearing*

The hill in front of our house
Was a maze of brambles, sumac
And twisted roots, which hid
The road, the trees, and the hill,
Like the tangle of bad dreams—
Forgotten in the first light—
That quietly numbs us,
Till my father cleared it
And stood alone on top.


## II   *Cider-Making*

The rasp of gears grinding
In the creaking press, the mash
Of apples clogging the cheesecloth,
The swash and swill of the juice
Sluicing down the spillway
And into the wooden tub. . .

Sticky-fingered, I stacked
The glass jugs filled with juice
In the rusted wheelbarrow,
Then waited for my father—I
Grew cold waiting for my father,
Who grew cold waiting for me.

III  *Root-Pruning*

He worked all day, digging
A ditch around the apple tree,
Slashing roots with his shovel,
Building a dirt wall around himself...

Dusk falling like rain, like leaves
In hard rain, I filled that ditch
With leaves, fine bark, topsoil,
Banking mulch against the cut roots—

As once, in the dark, he tucked
My blanket up to my chin,
Then turned away—to start new
Roots, stronger roots for winter.

IV  *Transplanting*

Those blackberry vines arcing
Across the path in the woods,
Tip-rooting in the grass,—

When I hacked at the stalks,
Gathering roots to reset in pots,
The wind lashed the canes

To my back; and when I picked
The rotting fruit, a globe
Exploded in my hands, seeding

These words in the air and the earth.

# In Spring

*for a child*


The trees hum in the wind;
And when the wind dies, birds
Fill the trees with song.
In the garden, pea-stakes
And sagging onions, stunned
By the hail and hard rain,
Lean in the same direction—
But look: the mustard's sprouted!

From year to year, we learn
What will root, what won't;
Why some birds grow silent
Before the sky clouds over;
And, once, words failing,
Why the grass whispered again.

# Epithalamium
*for Kitty & Leslie Norris*


Bearing the oil-soaked roots
Of a rose, a pair of shears, and a bandanna,
The gardener teeters
On top of the rotting fence, he slides
Along the slippery planks
Like a mountaineer hugging the steep,
Lurches forward and back
And, on the moss-covered corner post, stops.

He sways in the wind,
Trimming the crest of the hemlock hedge,
And laces the garden
To the street, and the street to the sun,
And the sun to the moon
Ribboned with ashes rising from the volcano,
In time for the wedding
Of the maidenhair to the mountaintop.

# Housesitting Poems

I  *Cowbells*

The calf's affected anthem; brass medallion
Of the wind; toll and sign of the sleepwalker;—
These necklaces of bells (bought at an auction)
Hanging from the handles of the double doors
May wake the blind before they reach the stairs.


II  *Carnival*

*Look: no hands!* cries the stripped clock as it ticks
(See the boy standing on the Ferris wheel,
Singing to the crowd gathered by the fence?
The one-eyed barker shakes his fist, believing
His son's afraid to leap) and tocks.


III  *Findings*

A locked trunk. Spoiled meat. Windowboxes lined
With mums and sleeping cats. Sunflowers sprouting
Under the bird feeder. Earrings embedded
In the lawn. A peach tree slumped by the garden, yanking
Its curtains down. This urge to look inside.

# Workbook

What became of the child
Whose stitches didn't hold,
  Who planted leaves in books?

---

Watch the trees slip out of their leaves! It makes them nervous.

They put their ruby leaves in a jewelry box at the edge of the woods.

Their yellow skirts drop to the floor.

---

When the widow pressed the white keys, the wrinkles in her face unfolded. She closed her eyes, smiled: her music drifted about the living room, brushed against the grandfather clock in the corner, and moved on. Then she shifted her weight on the piano bench and winced. Her hips, her gnarled fingers ached. She opened her eyes, grimacing, grinding her teeth. She played on.

---

Outside the window,
  Hidden in a patch of poison
    Sumac, books

Are burning—
  The blind man,
    Breathing the itching

Smoke, calls the vines
  Cascading down his trees
    *Dangling participles.*

---

Vines bending the buckeye tree—
　Two boys climbing a rope-swing.

———————

　Her song measured its steps across the room, charging the warm air:
the curtains yellowed by her husband's cigarette smoke wrapped
her chords in a shroud of ochre light before releasing them; the
radiator hissed and spat; the pie tin filled with water and balanced
on top of the iron gills bubbled, gurgled. Then, unaccountably,
she stopped playing...

———————

*Why did she leave?*
　I remember the grass withering,
　Seeds shriveling in the field, the chirr
　Of locusts heralding the fall,
　What I squandered of my birthright,
　Our covenant with the barbed wire...

———————

*Why did she leave?*
　I don't remember anymore.

———————

(The following spring, we spent a morning working in the rain,
cutting up the good wood and hauling the weed trees to the pile of
brush, rotten oak beams, and gasoline cans. And when the sun came
out after lunch, we rested on the leaves and branches spread across
the matted earth.
　—What are you thinking about? said my friend.
　An old woman, an upright piano, and three white roses.)

———————

Starting again, I wanted to clear
Everything: the weeds, the raspberry stalks
Ruined by root rot, the sumac vines choking
The buckeye...
                    But the stiff vines knotted up—
And, tugging free, I tumbled over backwards,
And felt the cool mud seeping through my clothes,
And the warm sun, and my body giving way...

———————

—What are you thinking about? said my friend.
The girl who laced my hands together with her hair.

———————

Waking at the sound
Of footsteps, I discover my books
    Fanned out on the floor.

Dusk: three bells,
And the widow sipping rum
    Till her hands stand still.

The plum tree's lost its feathers
—Whoever walks these slick white stairs
    May take wing and fly!

# Sentences

Ever since the nerve smoldering in my chest caught fire and fused my shoulder to my ribs, I've studied the weather like a sailor.

That sad young man limping through the square, lugging bundles of sheet music—where? What does he want from me? Why is his face like the sea? Snow batters his hair in waves of white and grey.

Here, look: my workroom's watermarks—driftwood washed up on the rug; ash dunes shifting in the grate; a spun-wire tree whose limbs glitter in the sun; dust; steam; the rainbow-colored sail . . .

And here: a necklace made of sandstone, charred juniper root, melted glass, and tailbone, welded together in a guildshop near Los Alamos.

Clouds washed over the trees, the wind spun out its tale. The red flag snapped to attention. The sea collected itself. And my kite, unfurling its wings, caught an updraft, disappeared.

This morning, tasting blood and smoke, I shook myself awake and huddled in the dark until I heard, like the sound of heated pitch exploding, you calling (again).

# The Street

At daybreak, in a snow-
White dress, it was a girl
Asleep under the trees.
Now it's the merry widow
Waltzing past in black.

———————

It opens like a coffin,
Or a book. It counts the words
On the last page, the seedpods
Left on the trees. It keeps
The footprints of the dead in line.

———————

Plot and measure; the belt
Our fathers used to steer
Us home; a dream, a prayer
Rising in our sleep, like bread,
With which to feed our children.

# Prayer

Here in the land of salt and stone,

Where the smell of rotting algae and brine shrimp washes over me,
rinsing my eyes and nostrils like the cold;

Where scrub oaks bleed in the hills before the bandages of snow
unravel down the slopes, and the last bees drift with the leaves

Into the canyon streams to shine with the stars;

And where locusts chirr in the saints' blood, and sea gulls fill
the holy square, and steeples lift their hats of smoke and haze
to greet the blind men singing in the street;—

I hear the clock's muffled drums beating again (like a child locked
in a closet, who pounds his fists against the door);

And so I repeat my prayer:

I believe in the wind lisping its hallowed song through the keyhole;
in the sound of the latch turning when my desk billows open;

And in the words, as the rug laps against the wall, that guide me
through the channel of the blank page

Out into the open sea.

# IV
# The Sea

# Nocturne

No one sees the woman kneeling by the bed of crocuses at dusk.
But she fingers the petals—the white sheets—nervously, waiting
    for the street to empty.
After the last bus sputters past, she takes off all her clothes,
    and hides them under a juniper.
She climbs into her flower to sleep.
She slips into her yellow nightgown, straightens the collar fringed
    with orange, and smiles.
When she pulls the sheets up to her chin, they become sails—
    they gather the wind whipping across the Sound.
She closes her eyes, and dreams.
The song of the flute in the house next door lulls her to sleep,
    even as her ketch, this flower, sails across the night-sky.
In the morning, in the harbor, the sun beats down on the water,
    and her sheets unfold as if by themselves.
She opens one eye.
Mist rises from the grassy leaves surrounding her, dissolving
    in the wind.
She stretches her arms above her head.
The first bus stops at the light down the street.
A blind man by the juniper listens for the roar of the bus.
She climbs out of her flower, leaving her nightgown behind,
    and disappears before the bus arrives . . .

One evening, a man comes to this flower bed, and sees a quilt
    of violet and yellow and white folding in on itself.
And when the sun drops behind the last house on the street,
    he kneels down in front of one white crocus.
And he touches its petals when no one's looking.
Soon he falls asleep on the wet grass.
And he sleeps through the night.
And then he wakes at dawn as on his first morning at sea—
    the wind in his eyes as he walked the slippery deck;
    the taste of salt on his tongue, like his first kiss;
    the sun burning his lips when he found himself alone.

## Still Life

She wants to keep the light
That spills into her kitchen, covering
The table everyone has left,
Is leaving, and always will be leaving,
That lulls the objects in the leaded window
To sleep—the rose shriveling in a beer bottle;
Her lover's sour joke: an orange
Shrinking into itself, its ochre peel
Hard as a clamshell; and a
Black banana,
The old moon wrinkling in the sun;—
So she splashes yellow oils across her canvas.

Soon the fruit loses its smell,
And the jade plant sheds its leaves,
And the last candle melts into its holder.
Then she's crying again: the light
Puddles around the empty table
That frames the picture.

# The Dancer

She flies to Reno once a month
To see the full moon. Under the sky-
Light in the hotel lobby, she waits,
Empty-handed and alone.

But when the moon appears, and she
Kisses the new doorman, and her eyes
Turn into lemons while her clothes
Drop to the floor, the old men cry,

*Eighter from Decatur!*
*Little Phoebe's here again!*
Bells ring, lights flash, thousands
Of coins spill out of her mouth.

Stuffing her purple underwear
In his coat pocket, the doorman
Slips out the door and hails a cab
To drive him to the desert.

Seven old women leave their own
Slot machines and, scooping the coins
Up off the floor, reinsert them
In her body, through her seven slots.

She starts to dance around them, pointing
At the moon, smiling. Blackjack tables
Empty. Roulette wheels, like tires, roll
Down the stairs. Crap shooters load

Their guns and hide behind the bar.
Stunned into silence by her dance,
The people sway in the moonlight
Till the manager arrives.

Then the old men cry, *Captain Hicks!*
*Captain Hicks!*, and the old women
Clap their hands, and the crap shooters
Fire at the windows and chandeliers.

The manager clicks his heels.
He knows her whole routine by heart.
He calls her husband, etc.
And she takes the next flight home.

# Indian Song

After the dogwoods blossomed
In your Indian song, your words
Became rain clouds scattered high
Above a Sioux plain somewhere
In South Dakota. My storm
Began in summer, and I
Chanted your new hymn: I am
A tall white woman, who's not
Afraid of the rattlesnakes,
Nor of the falcon's talons...

The dirt road to our house turned
To mud before your last words
Of love died... Now I've grown
Lazy with reading this foul
Night, thinking: if you were still
Here, still winding those petals
Through your hair, and if I could
Believe in you, I'd tether
A songbird to my armchair,
And spit this venom at the sky.

## The River

Once the storm died down, flocks of blossoms gathered
By the mud-clogged river, the crowd inside
Me knelt in prayer, and I watched you march away.
Soon the clouds returned their verdict, and the crowd
Regained its sense of place, its overweening
Pride, and the river disappeared. . .
                                        Now I wile
My tongue-tied nights away, considering
My leavings: molehills, chickweed, a glass bowl
Of stiff, white feathers—my charts of the wind's remains.

# Autumn in San Francisco

So late in the fall!
A woman hangs her sheets outside,
   And gulls pucker the bay.

Eucalyptus leaves
Stuff the gutters above us—
   Are you listening?

More wine! More wine!
The hiss of rain in the fireplace,
   The record that we scratched.

Fog horns wake us at dawn—
Mist shrouds the Golden Gate Bridge;
   A grey ship slips past.

The sweet scent of your hair
In the afternoon sun, and a blind
   Dog brushing the railing.

The mallards on the pond
By the Palace of Fine Arts
   Will never leave.

## Morning Song
*for Lisa*


When the wind in the water garden
Rises, like the woman who climbs the chiseled steps
(Expecting nothing), hummingbirds flutter down the ledge
To usher in the light of the indolent sun,
Lotus shift their weight, as if to stay
Awake, and the white lilies open
The eyes of the dead, until she lifts her hand
To test the wind. . . Then a sparrow
Squeaks, the water hums, and the reeds pipe and sway.

# Love Songs

## I  *A Covenant*

Smoke curls around a tree
Like rope. An old man sighs.
Then a woman ties the rope
To a branch, and they swing
With the ashes in the wind!
Leaves, like watches winding
Down, spill out of their pockets,
Feeding the fire that will carry
Them to the top of the tree,
Curling around them like a rope.

## II  *Nocturne*

When the luna moth—clinging
To the ceiling; to the arc
Of the porch light, like a ring
Of clouds around the moon;
To the memory of the moon,
Which is the song of the woman
Upstairs, naked and alone;—
Flutters its wings, the sky
Trembles above the mountains,
And the woman starts to sing.

## III  *The Dance*

Now the empty music stand,
Like a mannequin awaiting clothes,
Pins, and the dressmaker's hand,
Needs the bars and staves of song,
The tablature of joy and grief,
And quick hands, sure hands,

To build—each night—the cell
In which the lovers dance,
Dance until it's time to flee
Down the long white sheets of sleep.


IV   *Moonward*

In the bathhouse, asleep
By the leaking shower, the lover
Dreaming of the moon: when it drops
Its necklace through the skylight,
The moulting rug slithers off;
When it throws its shirt
Over the chair, the windows
Shiver; and when it cuts the rope
Anchoring the house to the earth,
The lover drifts away. . .


V   *Aubade*

She turns away, as a lily
Stretches for light, her arm dangling
Off the bed, her long fingers
Curling into a fist, and reaches
—In sleep—for the window. . .
Yet he remembers how
They lashed their worn bodies
Together by a tree, building a raft
To float down the river
Flowing through them to the sea.

# By the Sea

Beyond the warning sign
Swaying in the loose sand;
Beyond the guardrail that hugs
The bluff, the slick stairway
Down to the sea; and beyond
The sunken/sinking wall
Of weathered logs, of felled
Cedars and spruces that slipped
The clutter of the mill
And drifted through the Sound,
Breaking water till waves
Herded them into shore,
Where workers hauled them off
To build this barricade;
—Beyond all this, the lovers
Huddle in the wind, tending
The clumps of beach grass
Clinging to the last swatch
Of land, to the eroding
Cliff that moves beneath them,
Shifting its weight
Quietly, like a woman
In a rocking chair—
In the house by the sea—
Nursing her child at dawn.

## The Sea

The leaves scuttled across the roof,
Because it was autumn; because our house
Lay in the deep shade of maple and oak;
And because I chose the word *scuttled*, thinking
Of the rats who scampered through the cages
And corridors of dream last night, and of waking
At daybreak—alone...
                              And because you left,
The leaves scuttle across the roof,
The empty house whispers, *Fall, fall,*
And I smell salt air, and the sea.